MOON ROAD

SOUTHERN MESSENGER POETS

Dave Smith, Series Editor

ROAD

POEMS

1986–2005

Ron Smith

LOUISIANA STATE

UNIVERSITY

PRESS

BATON

ROUGE

PUBLISHED BY LOUISIANA STATE UNIVERSITY PRESS
Copyright © 2007 by Ron Smith
All rights reserved
An LSU Press Paperback Original
Manufactured in the United States of America
FIRST PRINTING

DESIGNER: *Amanda McDonald Scallan*
TYPEFACE: *Whitman*
PRINTER AND BINDER: *Thomson-Shore, Inc.*

The author is grateful to the editors of the following periodicals and anthologies, in which these poems first appeared. Some poems have been revised since their first appearance in print; some titles have changed: *Ascent:* "In the Old City" (Spring 1997), "Autumn Drab" (Fall 1998), "An Unexpected Aqueduct" (Winter 2003); *Blackbird:* "Greece" (2002); *English Journal:* "Because She Loves Me," "Yair Shows Us the Holy Land" (both 1997); *Georgia Review:* "The Teachers Pass the Popcorn" (Fall 1999); "There Is No Ferry," "Hotel Bellavista, Otranto," "Duomo," "Rain and Amaro," "Brindisi," "Moon Road," "The Media II," "Ithaca," "At Phorkys," "The School of Homer," "Palace," "Aetos," "Marathias Plateau," "Under the Greek Stars," "ΛΟΡΔΟΕ BYPON," "Lunch," "Sami," "Media II: Back to Brindisi" (all Summer 2002); "'Queen of Highways,' She Said—," "Getting the Hell Out of Dodge," "Funneled into Terracina, Which We Find," "Finding Terracina," "Fooding," "Monte Circeo," "Fondi," "Postcards from Terracina," "Museo: Grotta di Tibério, Villa di Tibério," "Santa Maria Capua Vetere" (all Summer 2005); *Greensboro Review:* "Great Granddaddy" (Summer 1986); *Journal:* "Approaching the Great Divide" (Spring/Summer 1989); *Kenyon Review:* "Learner's Permit on Skyline Drive," "Repairs" (both Summer 1990); *Kestrel:* "High above Terracina," "I Stop the Punto," "The Pontine Marshes" (all 2005); *New England Review:* "The Southern Poet Reads Emerson" (Autumn 1988); *New Virginia Review:* "Treehouse Poem" (Fall 1988), "The Soldiers Caught the Boys near the Top of the Hill," "When I Was Eight" (both Fall 1989); *Poetry Northwest:* "Sleeping on the North Rim," "So Long since I Have Put My Hand on You with This Pleasure" (both Winter 1988/89); "Epic" (Spring 1997), "Son," "Objectivity" (both Autumn 1998); *Ravishing DisUnities: An Anthology of True Ghazals in English:* "Finally" (2000); *Southern Review:* "Sickle" (Spring 1997), "Jet Lag," "Pat O'Brien Knocks Me Up" (both Fall 2000); *Tampa Review:* "Lamartine at Jerusalem" (Fall/Winter 1997); *Verse:* "Washington County, Georgia, 1941" (Summer 1990); *Virginia Quarterly Review:* "Henry James and the Future of Photography" (Summer 1988).

Library of Congress Cataloging-in-Publication Data
Smith, Ron, 1949 Feb. 2–
    Moon road : poems, 1986–2005 / Ron Smith.
       p. cm. — (Southern messenger poets)
    "An LSU Press Paperback Original."
    Includes bibliographical references.
    ISBN-13 : 978-0-8071-3271-5 (pbk. : alk. paper)
    I. Title.
    PS3619.M5927M66 2007
    811' .6—dc22   2006039357

This book is dedicated to

JK,

to

Mamer,

and to

Delores,
companion in travels outward, inward, upward,

with all my love

○

I have never yet met a man who was quite awake. How could I have looked him in the face?

It is not worth while to go round the world to count the cats in Zanzibar.

—HENRY DAVID THOREAU, *Walden*, Chapters 2 and 18

CONTENTS

MOON ROAD

WASHINGTON COUNTY, GEORGIA, 1941

They're all there, lined up
as if for a family portrait, except he
is standing on the bus's first step,
like the photographer, taking in the line
of brothers' faces charged with light,

his sister, the corner of her apron lifted to her nose,

his daddy at the back, that faraway look
in his eyes, and his tiny momma,
black hair up in a knot, face a fist, walks right up
to his fresh-creased knees and spits,
"You *look* like joining the Marine Corps"

in breath sweet with Buttercup snuff.

He's not a boy, despite these cheeks
he must carry to war.
They've been over and over it, like combing
new furrows for a locket.
So he turns and climbs to a cracked leather seat,

and the bus bounces, erasing them

with pink clouds, erasing
the house with its sagging porch,
smudged panes, stained roof.
And then the fields, dark rust waiting for seed,
going away to the pine woods,

the gears smooth after their grinding and whining.

REPAIRS

Words slipping in Christmas whiskey
like gears stripped, the old corporal gives us
Guadalcanal and my father, a boy, taking down an M1921
water-cooled machine gun by starlight, no moon,
while a voice breathes, *Marines, you will die tomorrow,*
a few feet away. Silently he places the parts
on a captured battle flag, its Rising Sun invisible
in the dark, and cleans them and has them back together
when the charge comes at daybreak.

This is the version the buddies keep alive

I pour scotch the color of oil
and tell what I remember of weekend repairs,
stuck bolt seethed at, ditch root cursed,
those narrowed eyes that sent me running
for a better tool in the apple pie order of the shed,
eyes that hated everything
that needed fixing.

I tell it. And feel the past moving behind my words, turning
like a man in sleep.

On the porch, through the white smoke
of our good-byes, our best wishes, when I squint I can still
make out the dry seas of tonight's full moon. It shines
on Mother's annual cry, her annual apology
for going on and on about things she cannot change.
She helps me kill the scotch. We hug each other down the hall
to the door she locks.

Sag of my old bed drifts and throbs like a square plywood boat
fighting swells.

His autographed photos of boxers
line up along the shelves he nailed for my books.
Nobody wants to be a grease monkey, he said
when I was man enough to swallow his sour mash.

2

We drank to the diploma he imagined hanging
on the kitchen wall. A new year
rattled the window with sleet.

In the moon-smeared ceiling he drops the washer

                    next to my truck and sits
and follows its zero with his eyes across the concrete.
The twisted hands in his lap are grease-black as the one
I hold out to him, the one he waves off. The one
that has never been sure when threads say that's enough,
that's perfect.

When I kneel for the part, the soft earth stinks and the night
is full of whispers.

                    Because he has come to help me,
he puts the hot cinder in my palm, something that fell
from those strange constellations. I place it smoldering
on the cloth, lean now to this scatter of dark machinery.

SON

O, she says, O, but doesn't
intend that sound that owns
her lips completely, all
she wants swallowed
by the event that keeps meaning
circling the singularity
of its own darkness.

Two years ago she was all bright
words and a strong back.
She lugged that chunk
of rosy granite from
out by the noisy road to
this quiet corner of her now
overgrown garden where he
can never stay long enough.

Between flights he pours
his hopes into her and she
says and says and says
nothing but her lone vowel.
Can he see in her eyes it's still there
among luminous clusters
of the past, nothingness
whirling its gigantic shadows?

Last month she pretended
he entertained her all Sunday
with his old armillary sphere,
turning the rings idly
while he talked a steady stream
about parsecs and black holes,
ephemeris time and his new
altazimuth. They told him no

body knows what registers or how.
Right now he's saying his hand
is the trellis and hers the vine,

but seeing, really, finger bones
slowly uncovered and disentangled
by some patient toothbrusher
of dirt. Yesterday she made

a fool of herself, simply howling
her O till it was ragged,
pulling him to her bony chest
as if she wanted to smother him
into the vortex. How can he think
he might somehow still be
her future waiting to tear forth
and gulp the air? How can he go on

vowing they will both,
in the so-called fullness of time,
fill it with articulate cries
and light, light banter about the bees'
headlong love of the azaleas,
about the stubborn earth's green,
relentless reaching for the stars?

BECAUSE SHE LOVES ME

Because she loves me she makes me say,
It's four o'clock.
Because she loves me, she says, No,
we can wait a while.
I mix two bad Manhattans and drink them
at the kitchen sink.
Back on the screen porch, she still loves me,
murmuring to Mother
who's too depressed to look up
from that dead hand
in her lap I dangle two cherries: You
are getting sleepy. You
have those, she says, eyes searching
Mother's face like the face
of a wavering lover. Hearts pop sweet
off their stems. Cicadas
ring the property with a mesh of anxiety.
She loves me
so much I say, It's four-thirty, It's twenty of,
It's quarter of.
She kisses everybody slow, moves slow through
the kitchen fluorescence, stops
at the wall phone to punch in two good-byes.
We love you, too,
she's saying, finger in her ear
against my yelling,
sneering that look that says, You don't know
about love. Because
I know about time doesn't mean I don't
know about love,
I'm saying, seeing through the roof a silver glint
scalpeling the sky, smelling
another sour night in the narrow bed
across the hall from them
as they toss in dreams of chasing me
under the gray beards
of the water oaks where I streak toward the traffic
and disappear

into the dark hair of a woman, any woman,
who holds me shaking,
who says, We can miss that plane,
we've got all the time
in the world.

GREAT GRANDDADDY

I remember his displeased face in the coffin
        the only time I ever saw it, the face
of all those whiskey-smelling, laughing uncles,
with the mouth turned down, the jaw pushed back.

The gravestones blasted my eyes in the sun,
        dazed me at the edge of the weed-ragged hole.
The grownups dripped sweat. Granddaddy twisted his brow
up there near the white sky. I couldn't breathe.

It looked so cool in the hole. The silver box
        went down. Why, why, why, said Brenda, her face
stuck in the neck of her new, red-cheeked husband.
On a stick David swung a dusty snake he said

he'd killed in a blackberry patch he wouldn't show us.
        His dress shirt stained purple at the pocket
over his heart. Under the big shade tree
by the white church Uncle Haskell sat on a root

setting his hand on fire with lighter fluid
        for the children. He smiled
at the identical flames flickering in the wide eyes.

TREEHOUSE POEM

He shook me awake on my vacations,
> and we thwacked sixteen-penny nails
> to the flush dent of the hammer head.
Clear drops seeped from green, salt-treated boards.
> We sanded every edge, smoothed every splinter away.
> Each second August we climbed
a higher tilting level. We made the crow's nest airy
and secure and big enough for me.

> But he's bulging into thirteen, sleeps late,
paces off this summer on the streets. And the oaks
> have swollen, are pulling the nail heads through
the 2 x 4s. "Good grief," he says, "it's only a bunch of wood,"
> face distorted as if by thought.
> "The first floor gaps," I say, "where we didn't plan.
The whole frame trembles when I raise myself
> onto the first rung." "Then don't," he says, smiles,
and the screen door slams.

> Last summer, swaying
in a creaking breeze, we passed the chimney.
> He doesn't even ask why we can't go on,
> up the trees as they grow, living in the highest
finished story, making the next slowly
> in the green and golden light, savoring
the smell of sawdust, *glad* for the growth
> that shucks the lowest level.

> He should say
> we could live on acorns and flying squirrels,
could watch the neighbors frown down their sidewalks
> to work. We could talk all night, putting words
> against the steady thud of cast-off lumber
> on the dark earth farther and farther below.
I say, "My daddy never did that for me,
never took me down the Savannah River
> in a canoe the way he promised."

9

"Polluted,"
he says, "I saw on *60 Minutes.*"
"This is real life," I say, "and you talk like
it's a goddamn sit-com." "I wish," he says.
"Nice talk at the table," his mother says, cutting the bread.
"Make it a poem," she says sensibly, "and forget about it."

LEARNER'S PERMIT ON SKYLINE DRIVE

We sit in back
where we can't be caught
in the nervous eyecorner.
Four hands in her lap,
one knotty ball. My fingers
have been numb for miles.

This is where we first learned to let go.

And our son is taking us again
along the spine of the Blue Ridge.
The Olds drifts to the solid line
white as a cloud, grinds in the gravel
next to a low stone wall
we will have to leap or penetrate
to fly into the valley.

On the road is all I will let myself say.

October, the leaves all golden,
the 5 p.m. light golden and clear
in the windshield. A net
of purple finches
starts from the roadway
as we swing from a curve.

He slows to 30 on an uphill, hurtles to 50

down and into a turn I know
will be our last. *Stay on the road!*
she whispers as tires float to the grab
of shoulder. Across the valley the mountains
soften to gray folds.

His frightened eyes in the mirror see only the blacktop
snaking, falling, rising beyond
the hood. *Just relax,* I say,
my heart unclenching, settling in

for the mistake
that changes everything.
It was October then, too, but cold
and dark in the big Chevy. *No*, she said, *no*,
and what did I say but *yes* and *yes*,

as if either of us knew the difference.

GREECE

Mountains, everywhere mountains,
young, soaring, jagged mountains,
where we are so
inconceivably old.

And sea, flashing sea
at every hairpin, glinting blue,
green, aquamarine
beyond the cliffs, lapping

the harbor, loses
its color at your feet, perfect
lens for the black anemone,
chloasma pebbles, quick, silver sardine.

And, oh, the goats! goats
in the road round the bend,
piss-luscious goats
that climb trees at our approach,

ashamed I come as a man,
not the Great God Pan,
and you, still-lovely you,
no nymph. Leathery goatherds

fixing us with that Orthodox stare,
rock ready in the hand behind
the back, goat pens, fieldstone sheds,
corrugated tin

rolling its distant thunder,
every gnarled olive shaking its basket
of cicadas, playing, playing
the hot, incessant, carnal wind.

AUTUMN DRAB

Even the sassafras withholds
its scarlet candles this year,
shows a few leaves the colors
of biscuits. "What good is dying
if it can't bring beauty?" I said
to my slim wife, who laughed
on her way out the door to jog.
Only the pokeweed, whose ugliness
my sickle spared in June,
lights the yard.

        Junk plant, gaudy
prankster, lusty hustler, it wears
its tacky ephemera like those women
I saw flying in the blaze of my childhood
who caught the trapeze swinging in my chest,
how they cocked their hips
in their tattered robes after the crowds
had turned their backs on the shadows
where my drunk uncle made me shake
those strong, horny hands.

        They smelled
like the depressed animals in the sad
little zoos along the road to Florida.
Under her thick mortician's makeup
the blonde had a greenish half circle
beneath one eye. The redhead smiled
black teeth that made rottenness
rise from some fouled cavity
below my heart, whispered

        of men
who liked to put their heads in
the lion's mouth, men the cannon
spit in a glittering arc against the big top's
loftiest darkness.

                    Bony Uncle Gus
winked anyway and promised to return.
I don't know how high he flew with them
in their muscles and sequins. I know
he went on drinking himself into a rich
stench, that appalling man who always
made me feel afflicted with the sacred.

But I was talking about this drab autumn
in our quiet neighborhood, the flameless
maples, the oaks the colors of dung.
And about the pokeweed whose bright leaves
already begin to curl and wither. "Soon,"
I say to my love, all flushed and breathless,
"all its black-wine berries will be gone,
its arterial stems, its vaginal magentas
vanished into a delicate frost glinting like stars
in the sky under our feet." "What," she says,
smiling, "in the world are you talking about?"

Hell, I don't know. My lost past?
Our diminishing future? "Look,"
I say at the window. "Right now,
isn't it something? Nothing
but pokeweed."

SLEEPING ON THE NORTH RIM

We had driven ourselves
all that way to be alone, start over.

      Now she wanted to talk. She talked,

but the wind wanted me to lie down and sleep.
She blocked out part of the sky.

      Yes, I said, I am listening.

The curve of her cheek: starlight.
Her words: rain that never reached the river.

      That was silence, that steady hum

of the engine swallowing blacktop,
that vibration in the body like utter fatigue,

      and the earth giving way,

breaking its vow, falling
into the long obscure story of its youth. Yes,

      oh yes, I am, I said, and I was.

HENRY JAMES AND THE FUTURE
OF PHOTOGRAPHY

My friend has not called. I send her poems.
She says she likes them,
though they tell too much about farm life,
too little about me.
When I visit her in the summer, she says
she hates her job, she'd like
for me to live closer, that she's afraid of death,
of the knotting of her hands.

She never says these things.
She sat on my sofa once, hair down in her face,
and smoked and said
she saw a kitten kill a seven-foot rattler
in the Utah desert.
I smiled, knowing her lies. I knew
it was a lie I'd give back
another late night. I'd look up from a busted poem
and smile

and drop her a line
about the blacksnake I found in the barn
climbing the shovel handle.
Seven lumps the hen's eggs made
disappeared
one by one as the snake squeezed the wood.
And then the snow,
a bear licking the raised
red metal flag,
putting his nose in the mailbox,
sniffing the letter,
the poems about the slugs mating
and the hummingbirds,
the postcard of Henry James glaring at this future
he's glad he'll never know.

Nobody gives a damn anymore
that Daisy Miller got it in the Coliseum.
James sits stiff in the past,
looking the insult of the lens square in the eye.
My friend will smile,
rub her spotted hand over her ruined face, stare
through the misted panes, draw deep
on a cigarette, not writing me again, not calling,
tracing a circle on the glass.
Emerson. She'll take down Emerson. She'll try him again.

OXFORD

I. Jet Lag

That first flight I did everything
wrong, skipped two meals, downed
two bourbons, then coffee,
coffee, coffee, and read cover to cover
a thick guide to Oxford. All around me,
open-mouthed bores snored. Off
the plane, on the train, English cows
whizzing past on English hills, taxi
to the tiny hotel *(charming!)*, and out
on foot to see the city of my dreams. I walked
until I knew I'd have to lie down,
which I did on my back beside a public footpath
in the gardens behind Christ Church.
I woke to a worried-looking tweed couple
bending against gray skies. It's too hot
for tweed, I thought, and closed my eyes.

II. Pat O'Brien Knocks Me Up

That first waking, naked, in the narrow bed
in the tiny room in The Parsonage, I found
a startled-looking woman backing out the door,
saying, "*So* sorry. I'm Pat O'Brien. I'm to clean
your room." "I'm all screwed up," I said,
pulling the sheet, "didn't get any
sleep last night, stayed up reading till seven."
"Oh, dear," she said, "and here I've just
knocked you up." It was midafternoon,
she was Pat O'Brien, and I, ex-linebacker,
had been knocked up. Abroad,
I was living abroad.

SICKLE

EAST END MAN SLAIN WITH SICKLE
—headline

"A sickle is a tool with a crescent-shaped blade used
to cut weeds and grass," the paper, for some reason,
tells us, who assume over our coffee that another
man was just plain murdered, not anciently slain.
You remember Herodotus's saying the Egyptians
harvested lilies with sickles, dried the flowers
in the sun and pounded their hearts into loaves
of bread, "baked," you find now in Macaulay's
dog-eared translation, "with fire." The paper
doesn't tell us why Horace Eugene Jones saw a flash
against the blue afternoon that bled his bubbling
words into the gutter, except to say he'd brought
the implement there to Tulip Street to scare a man
young enough to be his son. Why do I assume
there's a woman involved? There's nothing here
about why he threatened to lay down Albert Bray
like a clump of pokeweed or clutch of Egyptian lilies
or how Bray wrestled or tricked him or how strange
the thing felt in his uncalloused hand or how much
fear or joy either of them swung against the other
with this emblem of work and worlds harder and
simpler than theirs, than ours, than the reporter's
or his editor's who thinks, apparently, we've never
even known the clean sweep of such a blade,
the drag of wordless grass going down, of life giving
way to those who fill themselves with a beauty
that will keep them alive for a little while.

THE SOLDIERS CAUGHT THE BOYS NEAR
THE TOP OF THE HILL

What do we crackers really know about all that?

—a friend

It was scruffy, strewn with stones. God
has given us these stones,
a young man said last week. Now God
gave the stones to the soldiers.
Four soldiers, two boys.

The boys were made to sit,
facing the camera none of them knew was there.
One soldier displayed a stone
as if he wanted the boys to inspect it, smell it.
Another kicked them in the kidneys.
Again. Again. You will hear it said they were all boys.
I didn't see it that way. Maybe
it was the boots, the assault rifles.

One held up the fat boy's left arm and another struck it
with a stone God
had provided. He worked up to the shoulder,
then back down to the elbow.
A few blows along the forearm. Wrist, hand, fingers.
Then back up.

The foreshortened hill was covered with defenseless stones.
The other arm. The other boy.
It went on longer than most news shots. The boys
sat as still as they could.
They didn't try to crawl away. They winced, don't get me wrong.
They didn't beg. They didn't bargain. Stones
lay all around trying to look ordinary,
trying to look like stones.

EPIC

I.

The wrath, the hardening of the heart, the grief, the crushing
grief, the wild revenge, all the hacked flesh, river clotted
with blood, the whining gods, the handsome athletic men
unstrung, the panic, the shame, the stone certainty of divine
treachery, the feast of fatigue, the prisoners, the pyre, the games,
the fresh rage and the dust-impacted corpse, the night, the wagon,
the fearful hands washed by tears, the hard bread and the bitter
wine, the dark future lit by a thousand fires.

II.

The boy, the resentment, the wide world,
the man weeping by the sea, the man
pounded by the sea, the man crusted
with sea foam, sea salt, the girl,

the improbable stories, memories
aching like old wounds, the necessary
treasure taken for granted but never uncounted,

the familiar stony places, the arrogant youths,
the bright blood on the palace walls, the sulfur
and the washing and the terrified sobbing,
the dainty feet reaching for earth's relief,

the just bed, solid bed, bed full of words,
of man and woman fleshed unfamiliar by time,
finding ways back through each other,

the father bent in the orchard, sunlight
a blur of tears, the withered warmth
of the old man's embrace, the final babble
of angry voices, the sword hilt eternal,

even as the goddess freezes this gut,
that gut into frightened peace, the ready eye
undaunted, the sturdy gladness of the wily heart.

III.

A borrowed storm, the familiar
unfamiliar shore, much talk
of a future greatness,
the whole bloody story there on the wall,
the whole bloody story there at the banquet,
visions and searchings, etc., etc.,
and the queen is burning.

Thunder, the cave that's more than shelter,
but the tarred keel cuts through the water,
and the queen burns. Games,

the future presiding. One overboard
to make a point, one momentous
descent into the thick murk, implored,
snubbed, dubbed illustrious, fathered
not to make bronze breathe or words fly
or to measure the spangled meanings
of the night sky but for law and concrete
order, to battle down the haughty

and be them. Off now, to eat those tables,
scout the humble king's humble hill,
and kill, kill, and—that's right—kill.

APPROACHING THE GREAT DIVIDE

U.S. Route 36, June

Beyond the silos
it comes up,
that fluttering surge in his chest,
that whiteness only

last moment was cloud now
a palace of ice rising
from the plain and tanned women fall from it,
riding its slopes toward him,

their feet whispering,
bright winter clothes tight
as skin—then stopped, truly naked, pink-nippled
by a crackling fire.

Beyond this state
where his body would settle for sport
he knows everything
drops away to a place where

dead waters rise over nothing but salt,
a place where the boy his sister stopped chasing
dwindled into the desert,
where, she writes,

you can see God
in the wavering curve of the earth. She had
thumbed her way back to the lake's city side
and put on garments she would never, she says, take off.

He says he will never go that far.
He says they need no bodies
where they keep themselves pure
as snow, white as salt.
He won't look back

at the restless ocean of winter rye
that, yesterday, swallowed the house he grew up in.
He keeps his eyes on the whiteness

that comes up and up between him
and the sandbagged temple they wouldn't let him
in no matter how high
the waters rose.

To hell with them.
His heart beats
for this towering place between, this
imaginable frozen summer.

> And I saw the Holy City, the new Jerusalem,
> coming down out of heaven from God, prepared
> as a bride beautifully dressed for her husband.
> —Revelation 21:2

Lamartine, rich
with oil and garlic, arrived
exhausted above Jerusalem to find

Suleiman's golden stones
walling in the plague. Tented
with his laughing Bedouins

and their kissing dogs, he weighed
his life in one fine hand against
the nothing in the other.

Byron, he thought, would have entered,
groping for the fever that swells
like a fetus toward the blackest vision.

Lamartine galloped around the walls,
spinning the domes and spires
and minarets, making the only wind.

Outside his circuit, women wailed close
at new holes, keened far on hillsides
that were nothing but graves.

November sealed up the sky, shut out
the birds. In every direction graves
vomited ashes and waited.

What could he do but ride round and round proving
he was not a stone, a hole, a bloated corpse?
From inside the walls, the intolerable sound

of nothing. No cries of children or calls
to prayer or church bells. The nothing
was a sticky corpse stuck

in the stone throat of a god
like the sweet, gritty flesh of a fig.

SO LONG SINCE I HAVE PUT MY HAND ON YOU WITH THIS PLEASURE

> We must hold hard to this poverty, however scandalous.
>
> —Emerson

How distant I have been,
I see now, as clearly as I see
you stretching in this daylight,
winter white, touched by perfect black.
How sealed up in my sentences!
My narrow needs!

I let them go.

And here you are again, warm
under my hand, smooth
far beyond smoothness
of words, this curve
and sharp edge of hip

truer than anything I have said.

We could not start here, could
only return. But now we can
live this way forever, taking
nakedness with us when we leave
today this room of light,
back to the windowless spaces where

clothes speak, words are clothes.

I had shrunk inside my work.
But now the labor's over,
and this skin becomes me
and finds its proper place
in you, where I most fully am,
and no words wait to shape

this rightness, bareness.

Take me deeper
into what we come to
when we give up
everything for each other.
Forgive me, forgive me for thinking

I could live without you.

THE TEACHERS PASS THE POPCORN

When the mawkish Juliet
they'd come to resent
for mumbling began to wake

but the blubbering Romeo
didn't see her giant lips part, eyelids
flutter, fingers flex,

even they who said it was all about sex
endured a raw, unforeseen regret
that was nearly intolerable. And the darkness,

the jostling, whispering,
giggling darkness around them, stilled.
Breathed. Rustled.

Then shuddered through them like the massed
oblivious dead suffering a final
vision of the youth they had negligently been,

the salt and sweetness each
truly believed for a moment he, she
would never taste again.

OBJECTIVITY

The track star who hasn't done his homework
                  wants to argue again. His opinion
        is his opinion and mine is only
            mine. Yes, but, I say, there's something else, some
thing beyond mine and yours. We must strive for
        objectivity, I say. Perfect, like,
            objectivity, he says, that's, like, a
chimera. Chimera? You know: ain't real.
                  Yes, yes, I say, and yet you push for it,
        the way you push for the perfect hundred
            meters, the way you split the air to get
this thing that doesn't exist. It isn't
                winning the great sprinter goes for, is it?
        It's faster and faster, better and better,
            10 flat, 9.6, 9.2, 9 flat. Would you
        stop at 9 flat if you knew you could do
better? Sure, he says, but this is for his
            smirking buddies or the girl whose eyes keep
flinching from his tanned calves, his muscled neck.
        Of course not, I say, but now I'm talking
            to myself. Why bother to run better
          when you can never reach perfection? What
    is perfection here? A one-second race
            is twice as long as a half-second race.
Chop that in half, you've got that half left. All
        the eyes are tabulae rasae. A smile's stuck here,
            an actual yawn blooms there. You have to
         push for zero. And so we push and gasp,
            and go cold all over on the hottest
day, tear our lungs to the taste of blood. And
                  if we get it, the zero, we've lost it.
        A race that takes no time is not a race.
        It's the womb that wants to take us to death,
            I say, as the bell rings and out they go,
looking suspiciously over their shoulders
            at me and the weirdly perfect circle
I have chalked, from the doorway precisely
            centered, I hope, on my small, graying head.

When he reads Emerson,
he smells shit,
his own, and the strong urine
he's made since his kidneys
went bad. (Genes, blood pressure,
three decades of mostly mild
hangovers.) He loves Emerson

the way his granddaddy loved
indoor plumbing, the way he loves
his own body, his own
childhood, barefooted
on the rough/smooth railroad track
behind his father's house,
beyond his mother's perfect lawn.

The rough, he thinks,
looking up from the book,
is a ladder, is thick and black
and sweet with creosote,
or, splintered to brown, odorless,
is a cross to bear, a line,
another line, that ends and ends.

And the smooth is thin silver
going on forever under your summer
feet if you hold out your arms
like Jesus, if you're young
somehow and practiced, if you
don't think what might be

just behind you, outside
your mind's tight focus.
He knows you don't have to be
from Georgia to follow miles
of words sitting on a hole,

each line the solid thing
not there when the book feels seamless

to the final dot,
distant tunnel you can never
really go through. What,
he wonders, do others keep
in that small room
where he keeps *The Atlantic*
and his college *Nature,*

battered, its looping signature
no longer his.
When he's in that place
and looks up (he realizes now,
eyes lost in a honeysuckled fence),
he stares into a white hole just right
for his body, a space he's never

stretched out in because he's
one of those trained
by sport to stand for the body's
cleaning. He hasn't had a long hot bath
since his mother sat beside him
with the lid down, smoking, staring unhappily
at nothing. He'll never again,

he thinks today (stiff in his lawn chair),
feel at home in this skeleton
and blubber. "Particular
natural facts are symbols
of particular spiritual facts."
Bullshit, he thinks. Still,
he smiles.

FINALLY

My friend was finally going to write those poems.
The mortician asked me why he chose poems.

No money in it, he said. Why not novels?
The truly living, I said, can't close poems.

He'd done a few in his youth, quite fine pieces.
You can ask someone who really knows poems.

We had him burned. Then poured him on the rapids.
(Earth wheels fat narratives, but it slows poems.)

He himself the round world, Falstaffian, was
Suddenly Gloucester, blind, trying to nose poems.

Why toe the line? The crap of daily life can
Fertilize, at best, only prose poems.

He said to me once, Ron, you understand I
Should give up all this for sweet woes, poems.

VIA APPIA

"Queen of Highways," She Said—

and I: "More like Contrail of Roman Resolve
to Smite the Samnites."

In a light green Punto and troubled by not quite
remembered dreams (muscled limbs severed?
scuffle and bump, sticky darkness dangling),
we'd set out late in midsummer heat and slow
traffic on the G.R.A., slipped somehow directly
onto Via Appia Antica, rattled south a few miles,
squinting through the scrim of our bad night.

Every time we'd come, fewer relics along there.
Thieves, of course, but even marble returns
oh so gradually to earth and air . . .

I Stop the Punto

near a round tomb to take in the simple fact
that we are here, to see the close-set,
unmistakable stones, wheel ruts, umbrella pines,
jumble of remains under whitish-bluish
hardly-sky, what's here for the eye, what's here
for the mind: pavimentum, nucleus, rubus,
statumen, embedded diamond-cut of the silex,
gleaming vaults, splendidly pretentious monuments,
oxen pulling a jolting plaustrum, driver nodding,
more than half asleep, fiery-eyed lectica carriers,
smooth, shining with sweat, gauzy passenger
glimpsed curvy reclining, livery red and brown,
slapping sandals, unguents and armpits,
balsam and cinnamon in their wake, blank-eyed
tourists on their way back from Troy, Athens,
Corinth, Delphi, exhausted, but putting back on
their Roman faces, Roman erectness, this one
a philosopher, clearly, in his short cloak,
asserting, asserting, with his blackened walking stick,

lined face set to convey, if not contain, wisdom,
Milo and his clients hacking fallen Clodius
with swords and knives, quiet work for stoic,
fatalistic, pragmatic men, blades clicking, breath
whistling between clenched teeth.

Pass me the olives, Love. No, the green ones. And
a little more Frascati. What
did you see in my face? Why did you look away?

Getting the Hell Out of Dodge

Rattled down an increasingly rugged stretch
that's not on the map, turned back fearing
for our flimsy tires, over to Via Appia Nuova
strada statale #7, flung

                            through a maze of signs
missed markers honkingveeringbuzzingzoomers
of all sizes velocities angles of incoming Uturned
and were in bloody business with the insane
rest of the traffic slicing Ariccia's main piazza
slap down the middle past the doublebarreled
billboardblocked beauties of Albano and Nemi
over yeah that way blaring through Genzano now
Velletri I think impossible to imagine so far Dickens
finding only the sad the silent the sullen out here—

The Pontine Marshes

Suddenly the road unreels into freakish straightness:
la fettuccia, The Ribbon: after Cisterna it wiggles once

then zooms between rows of tall, tall umbrella pines
straight across what used to be the Pontine Marshes:

hypnotic: abandoned for a thousand years after the Saracens,
now again groma-straight for thirty miles: purposeful as a bullet.

Somewhere along here Forum Appii vanished with its crooked
innkeepers, drunken bargemen, faithful Christians waiting

to cheer for and cheer up Paul on his way to death.
Eventually a canal, maybe Horace's excruciation, joins us

on the right, the side toward the distant, glittering sea,
and runs with us, the past racing to flag down the present:

Hey, guys, wait for me! But I'm stupefied by jet lag,
poor sleep, this tunnel of pines, the brain-numbing fact

that we have no reservations anywhere and don't know
where we're going except down the Appian Way.

Funneled into Terracina, Which We Find

shabby, littered, supremely unpromising,
the Punto lurches up into the old city, steep,
narrow, blurring cobbled streets tangle—"*Not
a good place to die. Please* slow down."
"*OfuckingK.*"

Old Terracina eyes us, interlopers,
offers no hotels.

I loop back down into the new town, cruise aimlessly
for rooms, find none. It's hot, the car unairconditioned,
the town ugly, the time five o'clock, our bloated bodies
unexercised. I pull onto

a side street where I see some shade, where maybe
I can find a map in my bag, a map of this crappy place.
Delores, glummer and glummer, hisses, "It stinks here."
And I say, because just this second I see it:
"That's because

there's an elephant right beside you."

Uh huh: an elephant chained, poor fellow, by one leg,
eating the fig tree he's under, not ten feet from
her open window.

Like that rainbow over Selinunte
after the long, wrangling, unhappy drive from Agrigento,
that bickering, petty, travelers' misery, yes,

like that rainbow arcing toward rest and ristorante,
this foul elephant—trunk snaking dusty leaves crackling
into its shocking pink mouth—makes us adore everything
again, absolutely everything, even each other, even
the whole world's jumbo stench.

And in the Blue Guide I find—O Paradiso!—a street map
of this very place, backtrack to Via Roma, follow it
to the water and see

the Grand Hotel Palace, more than we wanted and
right now perfect, overlooking its own excellent beach.
And *there:* "impositum saxis late candentibus Anxur"!

Shower *and* tub. A big bed and a little balcony. Mm. Yes.
And *this* is a kiss.

Finding Terracina

Stuff dumped in the room, out to walk to centro storico,
both new and old city charming now we know

we have bed, shower, roof over our greasy heads.
Piazza del Municipio: old Roman forum with some

original paving. Duomo: dark, crumblingly lovely.
Republican temple heaved into the light in '44 by good

old-fashioned dumb bombs. On past much venerable
rubble and up into—in a few minutes!—countryside

along Horace's cursed three-mile upward creep. Below
and behind: that canal has gone golden. And that's

the Isle of Circe. And: harbors, Lago di Fondi, even
Fondi itself. Curve of shore around to, I'm guessing

again from maps, Gaeta. Bells, all through the olive grove,
bells unseen, bells moving, following us, I'd swear—

nymphs, let's say, improvising. "In thirds," my beautiful
wife sings, "like Chinese waterbells." On a hairpin,

inside a little shrine: photo of a young man smiling
on his red motorcycle; a piece of the very bike, splintered

fragment of a fender. Awful, we say, terrible, as an
Alfa Romeo whips past puffing a strong smell of coconut

on the hot air. We hike on, dripping, feeling more
and more alive.

High above Terracina

After the long climb past the gnawed-bone temple
in its ugly hole, past the musical olive grove
where the nymphs teased us, tracked us, snickering,
past the jaunty shrine to a young man's love of speed
and his red Vespa, at the top: massive foundations
of the Temple of Jove and a view to make one

weep: teal and gold and lilac and cerulean, sapphire,
topaz, indigo, turquoise, violet and emerald, pistachio,
pea- and bottle-greens: the whole Tyrrhenian Sea and
late sun and cypress and eucalyptus and that sweet
curve of the shore and somewhere down there a rank,
leathery elephant under a fig tree: a peacock pageant
of a landscape, sight the steady Roman soul, even
Horace's, could never feel the way we can: post-

Romantic, willfully sentimental. We make out

the perfect order of our hotel's rectangle of light
brown beach, chairs and bright umbrellas. So who's
this idiot with his back to the view wrangling with
a cell phone, every free finger punching holes
in the air? *Sì, sì, sì,* he cries, *sì, sì!* Why this deep,
sudden, salty kiss, all breasts and dizziness
on the crumbling cliff edge? Because nobody
on earth knows where we are? Nobody?

Fooding

In a tilting vìcolo hazy with skinny, evil-eyed cats,
we buy olives and wine at a tiny alimentari and
the old lady gives us a corkscrew, generous gift,
since I could buy everything in the place
with the meager contents of my pocket.

*

Perciatelli, linguine, spaghettini, vermicelli
at a ristorante full of locals, who try not to smirk
too much at how we eat our pasta, who never
cut theirs, never slap themselves with it, never
bite off something that falls back into their plates.

Monte Circeo

An island maybe once
but even then too close to the mainland
to hold free-range prisoners.

We've come to hold
our pig selves prisoner, straining to live
in the sensual moment

though still acting more like

fidgety Odysseus than his seducible men.
Past banks of oleander,

waterfalls of bougainvillea,
we climb in the heat forty hard minutes
to the acropolis, striving,

seeking God knows what,
finding the cyclopean wall soaring, yielding
our hearts to the green sea,

blue sea, bluegreensea . . .

Fondi

In that city of right-angled streets paved
neatly with ancient stones dirty urchins
cannonaded with soccer balls the boarded
up, overgrown façade of San Domenico,
where Aquinas Aristotled God, thundered
in that filthy corner of that hostile place.
Everywhere surly old farts on folding chairs
stared down the street, up the street, right
into your eyes. Where were their women?
Where were their teens? Very old, very
young stared with the aggrieved eyes of
those who hate living so far from the
beautiful, Bacchic beach, the meaningless,
restless, hot-breathed, heathen sea.

Postcards from Terracina

Our feet up on the balcony railing, Vespas buzzing
below us, the small harbor, a grove of masts, bristling
to our right, the Temple of Jove Anxur looking out
over our heads with calm, modern-looking arches
that are its many eyes, looking out to sea, over Route 213,
the shore road curving south beyond our sandals . . .

We sip cold Peroni. That's the beautiful topless girl
we put on our shades for and went down to watch
stroll the beach, that little sliver to the right of
the yellow umbrella, waist-deep in the foam.

Sperlonga's barely visible in the mist, way over there
where we have been today. I could tell you what
we found: the big black toad ("mort"), Sperlonga's
whitewashed charm, self-conscious quaintness,
its crowds of at least one French but mainly Italian
tourists, sun-dazzled walls, blue doors, narrow passages,
cascades of bougainvillea, peaches and plums haggled
over at the cart near the boat fountain, piazzas full
of gelati-lickers, scolding mothers, lovers sitting on
one another locked in those interminable, impractical,
and surely eventually painful kisses. It's mostly gentle
lip brushing, delicate circles, but they do it for hours,
hours and hours and hours. Even the purest love
can wear you out, wear you down.

When the gods bother to look at us, what do they see?
Caves? Dark holes in a world of light?

Museo: Grotta di Tibério, Villa di Tibério

Hellenistic marbles reworked, you could say,
         by Dark Age Fools:
                  "The (Shattered) Struggle with Scylla"
—shivery, delightful—
                  "(Busted-up) Odysseus
         Blinding the (Restored) Cyclops"—
Polyphemous gigantically there,
                  poker-faced girls
eye-level with an uncircumcised penis
         bigger than their backpacks.

The grotto empty now of all its treasures.

The villa stretching up the hill
        is simply a hill
                with a few scattered stones,
a little world carted off by the minions of time
        who will turn every Lexus
into trinkets one day.

                Echoes
        of ancient rumors: here
      Sejanus saved his emperor
            from falling rocks and started his climb
   . to disaster, here
the Laocoön original must have been, has
            not been found,
      may still be—

            if of course
      there ever was
           a Laocoön original—

Santa Maria Capua Vetere

Spartacus's stomping ground and the Roman Senate's
bull's-eye's just down the road from "Capua" (relocated
by Saracen slaughter). "Italy, without its killers, is feminine,"
Delores says. I remind her of the men in Naples (and
Florence and Rome) who couldn't keep their hands off
her or themselves. "See?" she says, filling her mouth with
blackberries we've picked from all around the fallen columns.
They're sweetened, I say, with dismembered gladiators.
"Oh, yes," she smiles, a tiny smudge of carnage on her lip.
We haven't glimpsed CNN or an English headline for weeks,
so the jokes are possible. "No, *necessary*," she says. Alone
in the vaginal amphitheater, wandering its animal pens
and locker rooms, we make rules: No talking about work,
no grieving over brothers in hospitals, sisters in rehab,
parents, friends in hospice or recently underground, brokers

deciding to fry or fly, bunker busters, baby killers, politics.
The burning question here's in the Mitreo: How
did they get a bull into that little sacred shambles?

An Unexpected Aqueduct

strides (you say), humps (I say) confidently (we both say)
across a field of soybeans (we guess together, laughing)
on to

      the site of Minturnae, where unarmed Marius
faced down Sulla's hired cutthroat.

                       Behind its theater
the old/newer/newest bridges separate time the way a prism
separates light, arching the River Garigliano,

                            ancient Liris.
Gusty, fresh winds blow down the Via Appia that marches
straight through the town like a column of soldiers, Main Street
between Republican and Imperial fora,

                        strongly assertive.
Fascist? OK, but happy fascist. *Diritto*, we say,
a jolly parade.

      We admire a calidarium and some latrines,
decipher inscriptions in the Antiquarium, invade a nearby farmer's
fields searching for the (unexcavated) amphitheater,

                    follow
the heart-full Garigliano, teeming with fishing nets and boats,
turn back finally

      for home (home?), dodge motorcycles and
Mercedeses, rushing into the sun to get as close as we can to Rome,
past camping villages and fishing camps and farms

                              and concrete
skeletons of housing projects awaiting funding and families,
past the sea, foaming and glittering off to the left.

                                Are those
my baggy eyes in the mirror, radiating wrinkes? Massimo had said,
You are not so young now. And you drink like an American.
Well, yes. We are

                       striving just now to stay superficial. But how,
really, did we get so old?
(Are we old?)

TO ITHACA

There Is No Ferry

You know is a ferry from Otranto?
The map is wrong, sì, and the guidebook.
You book a biglietto, a ticket here, in Otranto.

You cannot go, no, from that dock,
sì, where the boats nod.
You see: no ferry from Otranto.

You must go to Brindisi, to the end
of Via Appia and beg them
to give you the ticket I issue here, in Otranto.

I did not say ticket. No, I can give you
a prenotazione, sì, a letter. Ecco.
I'm sorry you have no ferry from Otranto.

The letter is for the begging
in the office just by Via Appia.
They will say Aha! un biglietto d'Otranto!

Via Appia is now a flight, you say, of steps and two
big bases for columns that walk away like legs
leaving sandals. A joke for the laughing, because no ferry.
But, sì sì sì I book you a room for tonight in Otranto.

Hotel Bellavista, Otranto

Everyone in town
has gathered on our balcony.
One a.m.? Tuesday?
The parco's trees are chattering,
kids are squealing. When do they sleep?
When do *I* sleep? The heat
follows me back into the narrow bed.
How can you snore
at a time like this? What sort

46

of time is it? Two a.m.,
near the Castle of the Loud Clang,
the park of the giggling trees.
A lone palm dusts the moon
launched from Albania,
falling now toward Alabama.
Three, four, soon
it will be time for a caffè and cornetto
and the long walk through the twisting
vìcoli I've always dreamed of
but won't tonight.

Duomo

We haven't really come to see
the floor. It's the rain. The Normans
made floors like children, wonderful
this violence, these misshapen men,
beasts with their wrong legs and extra
heads. And we certainly didn't come to see
the Chapel of the Martyrs, 800, they say.
You could probably count the skulls
in these seven towering cases.
Or the femurs and divide by
two. Please: No flash. Are you praying?
Counting your Protestant blessings?
Having yourself a minor swoon?
The executioner, the plaque says,
suddenly Christian when he saw
those untroubled eyes all in a pile
like fish eggs at the market, offered
his own albeit temporary head. And
here they are, 800 of them,
we'll take your word for it, waiting
in their individual horror-movie blandness,
their soaring collective jumble
for the oohs and aahs and clattering reassemblage
of Resurrection Day, clean as a whistle,

most of them, after 520 microbe- and insect-
and sexton-busy years, God's glorious Tinker Toys.
We'll skip the crypt. A little wholesome rain
will do us good.

Rain and Amaro

All day, side by side in bed
we read to each other
and drink the Amaro
we bought tipsy in Vieste.
Amaro Olimone,
we love you, with your
infuso di limone, arance,
even your *foglie d'olivo.*
We love your *aqua e
zucchero,* we love guidebooks
in bad translations, we love
the hard, straightdown rain,
each other, and especially,
Amaro.

Brindisi

Stuffed with vermicelli and watery wine,
we sit near the stinking harbor,
cabin booked, car safely parked,
we hope. Sunday. Brindisi
is empty. Fabrizio tells me
to watch the sky
for soapy water the housewives like
to dump on strangers.

You can see why
the Appian Way gave up here.

The harbor churns and stinks.
The whole world's before you,

I tell myself, bound for Ithaca,
sleep deprived, dyspeptic, crankily agnostic,
older already than Odysseus
when he plucked from his bow
that one pure note of homecoming
and doom.

Moon Road

A full moon disentangles
from the petroleum plant
as we pull out of the harbor,

rocking like childhood
toward Ithaca. Jets bank in and out
of an airport I've never seen.

The deck blooms backpacks,
sleeping bags, a few tents.
The ship shudders and turns, makes
straight for the moon.

We're riding the moon road into a cave.

We shake and shake our heads, but
it's still there, black tunnel
the moon mines paving our path with gold.

We climb out of the wind,
into our bunks, you above,
me below, rocked to sleep, chaste,
sky sister, tide brother,

light and dark, dark and light.

The Media II

The Media II rocks us south

toward Ithaca, the mainland
slipping by to my left.
Corfu was 4 a.m., some stars
strewn on the water.
Igomenitsa wore purple
and streaming dreams of rocking.

*

Now, the horizon's sharp as a knife's edge.
Nothing now but water.

*

That's Paxi, the man says,
and Antipaxi my head says and then,
Tell them the Great God Pan is dead.
A fighter jet trails a dirty tail
over the island. The deck below me
looks like Doomsday: bodies in body bags,
twisted faces, contorted figures tangled
among giant bolts, some moaning softly,
whimpering, like souls about to wake
wailing in the underworld.

Ithaca

... on the left, Kefalonià on the right,
the channel so narrow! Something Byron
could have swum from Fiskardo there, little village,
to inspect the island he thought
he might want to buy.

We rock past Polis Bay, Stavros
just a few houses above the harbor.

The single road cut high, high along the cliff
that is the flank of Mount Neritos

carries precisely zero cars or trucks, zero scooters
or bikes, zero hikers, zero
goats.

*

Sami's a strip of cafés and ragged
people waiting for ferries. Ragged like us.

*

The Blue Ferry round the south end of Ithaca—does
anybody live here? Rocks and bushes
plunge straight into the sea.

But: Vathi: Tiled and bright
hugging the harbor, hemmed
by a horseshoe of mountains.

*

Vathi's bay bucks and tosses all week
like white-maned ponies, restlessness
of youth, it seems to me, spirit
of the more innocent suitors.

At Phorkys

The cove at Phorkys is Dexia Beach
or vice versa. I read Homer
(Fitzgerald) aloud here
till my heart closes my throat.
Cicadas sing, cicadas fly all around us.
Steady wind. Sea-song.

Odysseus weeps and so do we.
Odysseus counts his treasure,
practices deceits on the scolding,

admiring goddess. My voice makes
the only language I know for sure.

This sun, these mountains, that sea-song,
sea-green, sea-blue, this woman
who's never, thank God, thanks
to all the gods, never had to be my Penelope—
she wipes away tears with the back of her hand.

The School of Homer

Archaeologists had left all their things
in situ, open notebooks (neat with penciled
Greek), stools, chairs, instruments, tools,
even their food hung up in the olive trees.
Rushes grew in "Penelope's Bath,"
though there was not an inch of water.

*

No place to turn the rattly car around.
Had to back up a quarter of a mile
in teeth-jarring rocks with my neck
in a crick and my ass Ionian wet
from the not-so-skinny dip I took
in the cold, seaweed-slimy water,
hopping from sharp rock to sharp rock
on the only beachlet I could find
on this end of the island.

Palace

Not too far from "The Field of Laertes"
I walked among the ruins of "Odysseus's Castle."

Near the road was a house made of fieldstone and
auto wheel covers, rocks holding down the tin roof.

When I got close, two goats climbed an olive tree
and turned their heads away as if they were ashamed.

It was morning. There were a few stones on stones
in a ditch and a little church to scare away the Great God Pan.

Didn't they know he was dead? When I think of it now,
I want to stand there all day and listen to the wind in the trees.

Aetos

It was July, too, when Schliemann came here
and became, they say, an archaeologist.
I take notes, know I'll need more
than a shovel to find what I'm after. I stand
on the shoulders of giants and thus can see
what won't work. The goats climb the trees.
They'll jail you for taking this one round stone.
The wind blows constantly. Bah to you, too.
We're all a long, long way from home.

Marathias Plateau

Sour yogurt on tasteless cornflakes, but
the sweetest honey—my Greek breakfast.
I have a new map. I kiss my bathing-beauty wife
and climb south past the cemetery.
"Is far," a woman says at a crossroads
still in the town, still in Vathi. Is hot.
I climb past olive groves and their
continuous cicadas. A boat chocked up
miles from the sea. I should carry an oar.
I climb, the road still asphalt, despite
my guidebook, stop for a scatter
of stunted blackberries, dry and gritty
in the mouth. Is very hot.
High over the sea, blue on blue on

aquamarine in a broiling wind, you can see
the mainland, shade upon shade of mist.

At Ellinikó the road goes rugged with rocks.
The rusted signs promise a cave, but all I find
are chickens, a donkey, not even swine.
One fieldstone hut, occupant nowhere
to be found. I call and call. Listen. Leaf-rustle.
From a tiny airline bottle I pour a libation,
drink a J&B to my dead, Homer-loving friend.
Way down there, I choose to believe
(with the guidebook), that's the island, little
more than a wooded wedge,
where they hid, the bastards, and failed,
and so died young. The sun is brighter now
and my water gone. I walk south
into more and more nothingness
till a wild pear saves me, a scrawny one,
its small fruit juicy and sweet
as a goddess's love. I go on and on
finding nothing but rocks and tough shrubs,
high above the sea, so happy I can't think
of a thing that could make me sit down
and weep for home.

Under the Greek Stars

Remember how we lay on the roof
of the Hotel Mentor, its "roof garden,"
and watched the shooting stars?
How the chambermaid nearly stepped
on us when she came to take in
her flapping underwear?
The sky wasn't really Greek, was it?
It was the sky. But it was diamond-clear.
And every shooting star said, Yes, oh yes,
Odysseus slept here.

ΛΟΡΔΟΕ ΒΥΡΟΝ

He looks out to the little Venetian quarantine island
where letters were smoked before his time,
before he came in 1823, to Greece,
to die. No stern Odysseus here
as in Stavros, no blank-eyed Homer,
just this sulky, very young Englishman
whose odyssey was *away* from home, away
from despised wife, on the seas hungering
for—what? Self, relief from disgust, the sexual
adventure Odysseus took for granted,
took and took, like that later lord, but who
unlike the self-sick romantic,
came to fight through to life, to live and love in health.
To our health, My Love. Let's drink to the morning,
to Ithaca of myth and Metaxa.

Lunch

Atomic tzatzíki, and that local rosé
they call red, the air all around us alive
with Greek and Italian that pulls us
this way, that. What
did she say to the boy? You are crazy
as a she-wolf?

Sami

Beside our modest monoliths of luggage,
we sip and read until the sun is tired
in the "ΟΑΣΗ ΚΑΦΕΤΕΡΙΑ."
The family has a new Etruscan roof,
I'd say, above its business, above its balcony
and shuttered cool. When I've walked off
my heartburn, I find you with a square-headed
thirteen-year-old ("and a half") at the table

next to the singer. Panagiotis Stanitsas
fetches vodka, fetches taramasalata, refuses
all payment, all tips: "I am the boss." He wants
to come to the U.S., but not to study "as usual."
Michael Jordan's what he wants to study,
hamburgers, baseball, basketball, which he plays.
We wave lira, drachmas. His father, suave, hassled,
says he is indeed the boss. My son give you. It's OK.
The ferry is always late, says Panagiotis.
Not before midnight. I tell you not to worry.

I worry. We roll our monoliths to the mole,
winding through the cars and trucks. We wait, shivering.

One a.m.: two ferries—no, *three!*—leviathans jostling
for the dock! Somehow, no collisions. The mob moves.
Two by two past the slot machines we climb and climb
to our bunks and our blessèd toilet. Too much,
it's all too much. We fall groaning
into dreams: long hikes, heavy burdens,
goddesses snickering in the amethyst cloud
above the silver olives.

Media II: Back to Brindisi

This boat is a dolphin
all night, showing its back
to the stars, whacking your ladder
next to my head.
I try to sleep, holding it all night
with my right hand. It's a spear.
My dead friend looks up
from his digging, looks up
into my eyes. He wears the small field
like an aura, the freshly turned field
ringed with ancient trees.
He is my astonished father, Laertes.
We're both crying. He can't believe

it's me, even though it isn't.
When they come, the angry ones,
we will fight them, shoulder to shoulder
and laughing in the gold-dust sunlight
high above that enameled sea.

HOLY LAND

I. In the Old City

"Right, that is the Call to Prayer,"
        the Methodist missionary who's down
for the weekend from Nazareth says
                in an Appalachian twang.
                                The azan
fills the dusty heat with mufti and myrrh,
        saffron tambours, sequined ciphers,
                        jasper lutes and jasmine monsoons,
whirl of quartertones: I'm trying to learn how to listen.

        Recorded?
                "Sounds *like.* You notice shops
on the Via Dolorosa're closed today?"
                        Yes, the mere hallway I've come to find
crowded clinking with cheap, perfumed exotica—
                hushed corridor of closed doors, eyes
                eager to appear friendly now gone,
the few drifting past glittering with suspicion, like these notes, these
        words my head cannot hold, a jeweled box
                sealed by the centuries and snatched back
                by the owner who thinks better of selling just now
                        to the likes of me.

        "Yeah, they close down like that when there's trouble.
        You won't read about it in the papers,
                but a Hamas boy got zapped in Nablus.
No trinkets today, no veronicas.
        So they cut off their hooked noses,
pardon my language, to spite their ugly faces.
                        And they turn up the muezzin's volume
                to irritate the soldiers,
but the soldiers is hard to irritate.
                        Loud, though, ain't it?"

Yes, loud with the wavering of God
        and the off-key, cross-key yearning

> to fill the flesh completely
> with the angry vacuum of deity.

I turn away, and the missionary says, I swear, "Ciao, compadre."

> Through Jaffa Gate, past some boys and girls who wear
black machine guns down their backs like ponytails,
> Suleiman's bright wall stretches itself in the late sunlight
> like, yes, a flaming sword
> between all the ancient prayers
> and the gleaming condos
patrolling the hillsides of the future.
> And down in the Gihon Valley at the traffic roar
> a man who might be dead already or sulking
> in the back room of his shop is still telling me over and over
> I am on the wrong side.

II. Yair Shows Us the Holy Land

Yair, our guide, "hates" Tel Aviv, its traffic, and Jerusalem,
> he says, is "a very emotional city," which is to say,
> he hates it, too. We love Tel Aviv this day, love
our beautiful waitress on Dizengoff, just out of the army,
> who smiles a shocking gap in her white teeth
> and brings more and more shishlick. Except for alfresco
and the ancient, momentous alphabet floating on the air,
> famous Dizengoff, lively sidewalks calmed by shaggy trees,
> two lanes jazzing between ordinary storefronts, is

Savannah, Georgia, when we were children, before
> crime had rotted away the city's heart. May we take
> the cardboard Maccabee coasters? "Why not,"
our waitress sniffs, tosses half a dozen onto the table. Yair shrugs,
> "We have not yet learned good manners—a young country."
> She strides away with Yair's purposeful gait, so unlike
the coy saunter of Savannah girls who cannot imagine
> their lovely legs blown into the tops of ficus trees
> one fine morning when a young man dressed handsomely

in apocalypse boards a bus and makes even his bones holy shrapnel.
    No, in Savannah the girls were killed by beasts we'd trained
        to rip their pocketbooks or their own sheer pleasure
from astonished screams. Back there, where red flecks in the trees'
      patriarch beards meant only tiny insects that wanted to live securely
        inside your skin, no one boarded our buses with death warm
against his heart that would separate his tissues for the dream
    of the cause, for the dream of the pure killing of righteousness
      unknown in our Savannah where people died

for all the wrong reasons, lived, we're dismayed to think just now,
    for all the trivial right ones. "We go," says Yair, pointing
      with that finger that's missing its first joint,
an unimportant loss, he says, for ten years in the service.
    He puts on his cowboy hat and marches us toward
      a garishly painted gurgling fountain whose metal rings
will begin to revolve after dark and sing, suddenly, Ravel's bolero
    in a whirl of lights and a spurt of flame. Yair will watch us gravely
      as we whoop and clap. He'll shrug his fortieth shrug of the day.

"Do I like it?" he'll say. "No. It's *art,* all pretty shape and passion and
    nonsense. One cannot speak of truth, only opinion."

WHEN I WAS EIGHT

you promised me
a canoe trip down the river
when I turned thirteen.

We never went, never

skimmed the brown water, leaning
on the river's weight as the gator
left his bank to pull the long tail

in behind like a memory,

or saw together the heron go whiter with wings
and lift against the marsh mist,
floated wordless near the slap in the reeds

of the gone ski boat's wake

where fiddlers came and went like anxieties
into the mud, took in all day the strong
river smell, came home sore in the shoulders,

dozing warm inside ourselves,

the cords and knots of our backs pulled
and kneaded by Mother's firm hands,
lay side by side on the floor, smiling

at each other's sweet grimaces,

deep sighs, said, After all these years
it was worth the wait.

NOTES AND DEDICATIONS

"Great Granddaddy": Dedicated to Haskell Purvis and David Purvis.

"Treehouse": Dedicated to Brooks Smith.

"Henry James and the Future of Photography": Dedicated to Shirley Anders.

"Oxford": Dedicated to Rosemary Pountney.

"Objectivity": Dedicated to Jim Hall and Neale Mucklow.

"Epic": *Iliad; Odyssey; Aeneid*—and dedicated to Stuart Wheeler.

"The Southern Poet Reads Emerson": Dedicated to Terry Hummer.

"Finally": Dedicated to George Ocran Squires and Agha Shahid Ali.

"Fooding": Dedicated to Sari Gilbert.

"Fondi": Dedicated to Massimo Bacigalupo.

"Monte Circeo": Dedicated to John Boggs.

"Museo: Grotta di Tibério, Villa di Tibério": Dedicated to Charles Johnson.

"Duomo": Dedicated to Irby Brown.

"Holy Land": Dedicated to Yair Keidan.